P9-CFT-866

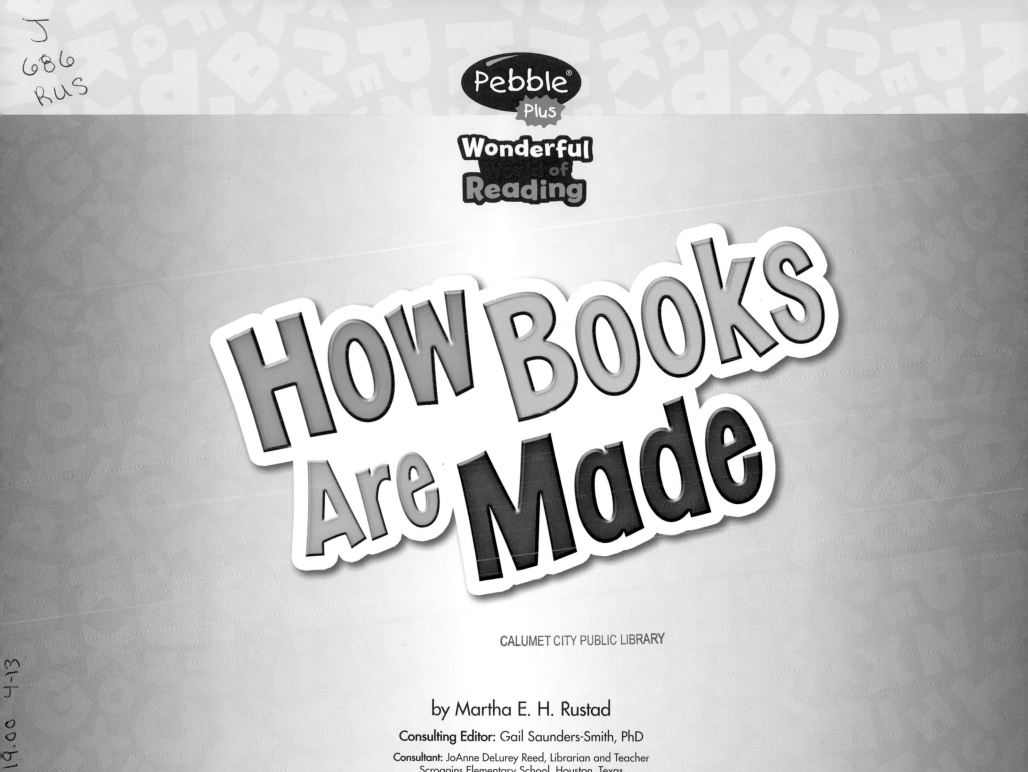

Pebble® Plus

Wonderful World of Reading

How Books Are Made

by Martha E. H. Rustad

Consulting Editor: Gail Saunders-Smith, PhD

Consultant: JoAnne DeLurey Reed, Librarian and Teacher
Scroggins Elementary School, Houston, Texas

CAPSTONE PRESS
a capstone imprint

Pebble Plus Books are published by Capstone Press,
1710 Roe Crest Drive, North Mankato, Minnesota 56003.
www.capstonepub.com

Library of Congress Cataloging-in-Publication Data
Rustad, Martha E. H. (Martha Elizabeth Hillman), 1975–
  How books are made / by Martha E.H. Rustad.
     pages cm.—(Pebble plus. Wonderful world of reading)
  Includes bibliographical references and index.
  ISBN 978-1-62065-095-0 (library binding)
  ISBN 978-1-4765-1739-1 (eBook PDF)
1. Books—Juvenile literature. 2. Book industries and trade—Juvenile literature. 3. Authorship—Juvenile literature. I. Title.
  Z116.A2R87 2013
  002—dc23   2012030346

Editorial Credits
Erika L. Shores, editor; Veronica Scott, designer; Marcie Spence, media researcher; Laura Manthe, production specialist

Photo Credits
Alamy Images: Blend Images, 21, David Young-Wolff, 9, ZUMA Wire Service, 19; Capstone Studio: Karon Dubke, cover (child), 17; Corbis: Helen King, 15; Shutterstock: Anastasija Popova, 5, Elena Elisseevaq, 7, Kovalchuk Oleksandr, cover (book), olly, 13, Quang Ho, cover (stack of books), wavebreakmedialtd, 11

Note to Parents and Teachers

The Wonderful World of Reading series supports Common Core State Standards for Language Arts related to craft and structure, to text types and writing purpose, and to research for building and presenting knowledge. This book describes and illustrates how books are made. The images support early readers in understanding the text. The repetition of words and phrases helps early readers learn new words. This book also introduces early readers to subject-specific vocabulary words, which are defined in the Glossary section. Early readers may need assistance to read some words and to use the Table of Contents, Glossary, Read More, Internet Sites, and Index sections of the book.

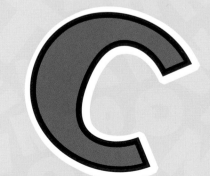

Printed in the United States of America in North Mankato, Minnesota.
092012   006933CGS13

TABLE OF CONTENTS

From Idea to Manuscript

One day, an author sees

a new kind of dog.

She wonders, "What is a

Cesky terrier?" She has an idea

for a new book to write.

Say it like this: **Cesky (chess-KEY)**

4

The author researches

Cesky terriers. She reads

books and Web sites.

The author writes and rewrites.

Now she has a manuscript.

The author wants people to read

what she wrote. So she sends

her manuscript to many publishers.

They make and sell books.

Most say no. But one says yes!

From Manuscript to Layout

An editor reads the manuscript.

He asks other editors to read it.

He asks a Cesky terrier breeder

to read it. He fixes mistakes.

He moves words around.

A designer works on how
the book looks. He finds
pictures of Cesky terriers.
He puts the words and pictures
together in a computer file.

From Layout to Printer

Editors and designers look over the file for mistakes. Then the file is turned into a digital book to read on computers or e-readers. The file is also sent to a printer.

At the printer, the book is printed

on huge sheets of paper.

Then pages are cut and

glued and stitched to a cover.

The book is ready!

From Printer to Library

The publisher tells librarians about the new book. Readers are asking for books on Cesky terriers. A librarian buys the book.

At the library, a boy asks about
dog breeds. The librarian shows
him the new Cesky terrier book.
The author's idea is now
in the hands of a reader.

Glossary

author—a person who writes books

designer—a person who decides how a book will look

editor—a person who works with an author to make the words in a book sound just right

file—a document stored on a computer; a book file can have words, photographs, and artwork

manuscript—a book that has not been published

publisher—a company that pays for a book to be edited, designed, and printed; the publisher then sells the book

research—to study and learn about a subject

stitch—to sew loops of string to hold something

Read More

Donovan, Sandy. *Pingpong Perry Experiences How a Book Is Made.* In the Library. Minneapolis: Picture Window Books, 2010.

Malam, John. *Journey of a Book.* Journey of a ... Chicago: Heinemann Library, 2013.

Rustad, Martha E. H. *The Parts of a Book.* World of Reading. North Mankato, Minn.: Capstone Press, 2013.

Internet Sites

FactHound offers a safe, fun way to find Internet sites related to this book. All of the sites on FactHound have been researched by our staff.

Here's all you do:

Visit *www.facthound.com*

Type in this code: 9781620650950

Index

Word Count: 239
Grade: 1
Early-Intervention Level: 23